D1505805

IS THAT A FACT?

Did Greek Soldiers Really Hide Inside the Trojan Horse?

And Other Questions about the Ancient World

CAROL M. SCAVELLA BURRELL

ILLUSTRATIONS BY COLIN W. THOMPSON

LERNER PUBLICATIONS COMPANY

Minneapolis

Contents

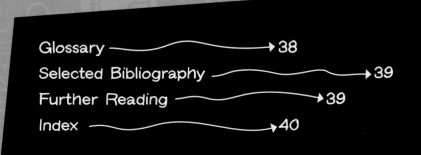

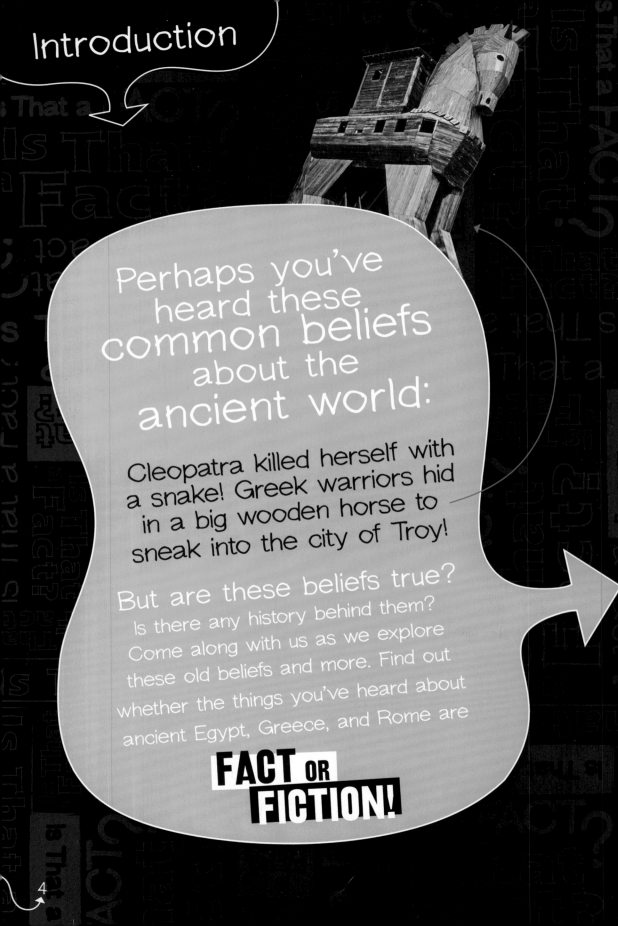

Perhaps you've heard these common beliefs about the ancient world:

Cleopatra killed herself with a snake! Greek warriors hid in a big wooden horse to sneak into the city of Troy!

But are these beliefs true? Is there any history behind them? Come along with us as we explore these old beliefs and more. Find out whether the things you've heard about ancient Egypt, Greece, and Rome are

FACT OR FICTION!

Did Ancient Egyptians Have Cat Gods and Cat Mummies?

YES! Ancient Egyptians thought a lot of different animals were important to the gods. But cats were the most important of all. Many cats lived in beautiful temples built to honor Bast (*above*), the cat-headed goddess. If there was danger, such as a fire, people hurried to save the cats.

Families loved their pet cats and wrapped them up as mummies (preserved bodies) when they died. Families carried the cat mummies in little coffins to cities where Bast was worshipped. Thousands and thousands of cats were buried in special cemeteries.

In return, cats did valuable jobs for humans. They kept mice out of the grain and chased away snakes. Egyptians liked them better than dogs.

This Egyptian cat mummy is from about 300 B.C.

Cats always seem so mysterious and independent. They come and go in the middle of the night. It's easy to believe that they see and know things humans don't.

Cat mummies were discovered in the 1800s. But people didn't treat the ancient finds with respect. Explorers burned cat mummies like logs to power the engines of their barges—the boats that traveled up and down the Nile. They were only cats, after all. That's the exact opposite of what the ancient Egyptians believed!

Did Egyptians Really Believe Mummies Would Come Back to Life?

NOT EXACTLY, but mummies were very important.

This is the mummy of Ramesses II. He was a pharaoh in the thirteenth century B.C.

Ancient Egyptians mummified cats, fish, birds, scarab beetles, bulls, and other animals. They also mummified people. They took out the heart and other organs and then scooped the brain out through the nose and threw it away. They dried the body for seventy days. They believed that people think with their hearts, so hearts were then put back inside the body. Resin, a sticky tree sap, was poured over the body. The resin dried into a hard shell. This was to make sure the body lasted forever.

According to Egyptians, the soul had many parts. If a person didn't take care of all the parts, he would forget who he was. The mummy was home base, like an anchor to keep pieces of the soul from floating away.

The Egyptians had so many different beliefs that they didn't all agree about what happened to a dead person. Mummies of wealthy people were buried with gold and other treasures for use in the afterlife. Some mummies were buried with a travel guide called *The Book of the Dead*. It told the soul how to pass the tests on the way to the afterlife. Egyptians believed that once

Mummy Medicine

In the Middle Ages (A.D. 500–1500), a hard, black substance called bitumen was used as a cure for everything. It came from Persia (modern-day Iran), where it was called *mummiya*. Travelers to Egypt thought the old, dry resin on entombed bodies was bitumen. So they called the bodies mummies. Ground-up mummy became a popular medicine.

people reached the afterlife, they faced a final test. Their hearts were weighed. If the person was good, the heart was lighter than a feather. The gods let the person into their lands, where he or she would live for millions of years.

In ancient and modern times, people have robbed tombs for the treasures inside. The mummies that were so carefully hidden are damaged or lost. All that was ever found of Djoser, the first pharaoh to be buried in a pyramid, is his left foot.

Is It True That Egyptian Royalty Were Buried with Their Servants— Whether the Servants Were Dead or Not?

NO. Lots of people believe this myth. And in some ancient lands, human servants *were* buried in royal tombs. But here's the story about Egyptian customs and beliefs.

Ancient Egyptians thought you had to work hard in the afterlife. This work included planting crops and carrying water to canals. It also included very unpleasant jobs, such as moving sand from one side of the Nile to the other. And Egyptians believed that the dead would have to do these chores for millions of years!

The ancient Egyptians believed servants could help mummies with all this work—and they thought they could send servants to the afterlife by burying them next to the person who had died. Very early on, they decided they didn't believe in burying *real* people. Instead, Egyptians placed special "servant dolls" called shabtis in tombs alongside the deceased.

Shabtis were made from many different materials, including wood, alabaster, and terra-cotta. The shabtis looked like small mummies. Their little hands were free so they could hold tools. Magic spells were written on the shabtis so they could come to life when needed.

The more shabtis a person could afford, the easier the afterlife. King Tutankhamen had 413 shabtis. But even very poor people were buried with shabtis. Mummies with a lot of shabtis also had to have boss shabtis to make the others behave.

In later days, Egyptians made shabtis that looked like regular people, not mummies. These shabtis were made for all sorts of jobs—such as baking bread, weaving clothes, and brewing beer. They made everything a mummy needed for the afterlife.

Some of Tutankhamen's shabtis looked just like the pharaoh.

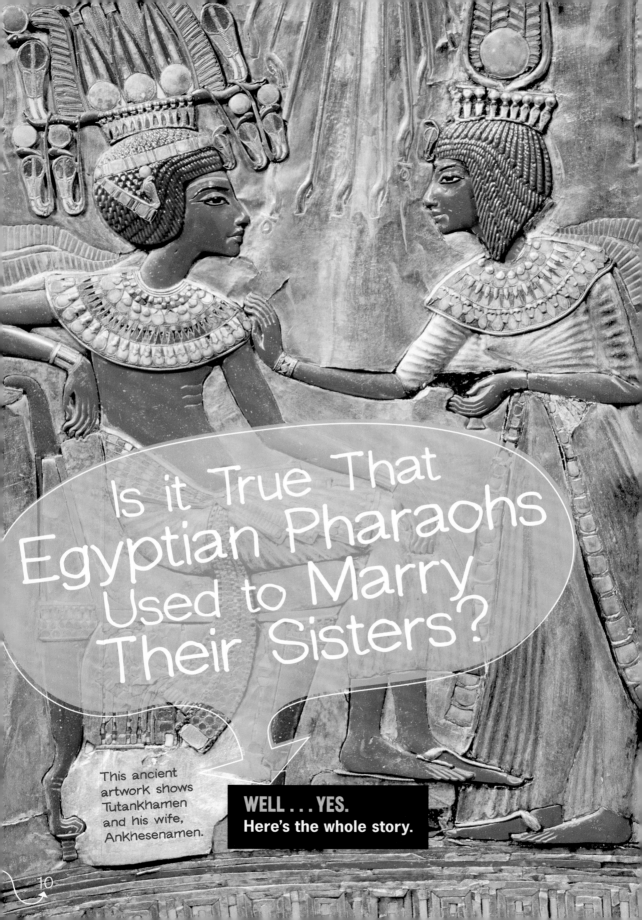

Is it True That Egyptian Pharaohs Used to Marry Their Sisters?

This ancient artwork shows Tutankhamen and his wife, Ankhesenamen.

WELL . . . YES.
Here's the whole story.

A man and a woman in Egypt, when they were in love, called each other brother and sister. They did this to show how close they felt. When ancient Greek historians wrote about Egyptian royalty, they misunderstood this. They thought that the couples were related.

But some royal couples actually *were* brother and sister. Why would a pharaoh marry his sister? Well, marrying a close family member would help ensure that no other family would get a share of the power. Pharaohs also often married other relatives, including daughters and nieces.

Pharaohs could have more than one wife. All the wives took up important positions in the royal court. They got the title "queen."

Other royal men closely related to the pharaoh also could have many wives. A prince might be married to his cousin and his half sister as well as other women. Figuring out a royal family tree can be next to impossible!

A pharaoh's heir might be his son. Or it might be his brother, his nephew, his cousin, or his half brother. Or his nephew *and* his son. King Tutankhamen's family tree is one of the most confusing of all. It's hard to say for sure whether he married his niece or half sister or cousin. Scientists continue to study records, portraits, and cells from mummies to find out.

The Father of History

The Greek historian Herodotus wrote about Egypt in the 400s B.C. By that time, Egypt's past was already ancient history. Herodotus is called the father of history. He always told both sides of a story. He traveled all over to look for information. We don't know about any writer before him who tried so hard to find out if an old story was a fact.

Did Cleopatra Kill Herself with a Snake?

YES, according to people who were nearby, including Cleopatra's own doctor.

The Cleopatra in question, Cleopatra VII, was Egypt's last pharaoh. She became queen in 51 B.C. when she was eighteen years old. Her family had ruled since the days of Alexander the Great, three centuries before.

By the 50s B.C. Rome wanted control of Egypt. Cleopatra teamed up with two Roman generals—first, Julius Caesar and then Mark Antony (in Latin, Marcus Antonius). She thought they could help her keep control of Egypt. But Caesar and Antony had their own problems back in Rome. They couldn't help Cleopatra. Soon Rome's new leaders made Egypt part of a new empire.

Cleopatra was caught in a hard situation. The Romans showed off their victories in a parade called a triumph. The winning general painted his face purple and rode in a golden chariot. Prisoners marched behind him in chains. For a queen, this would be too awful to bear. That may be why Cleopatra chose to kill herself.

Or maybe Cleopatra killed herself for love. She fell in love with Anthony when she joined forces with him. The two ended up getting married. When Anthony died in 30 B.C., Cleopatra was left on her own.

Whatever the reason, soon after, Cleopatra had a poisonous snake brought to her, hidden in a basket of figs. She let the snake bite her on purpose, ending her life. The snake might have been a cobra. Cobra poison is quick. It kills victims so quickly that criminals were executed by a cobra bite to the chest. Also, snakes were sacred to the goddess Isis. Cleopatra considered herself to be the daughter of Isis. A snakebite was a way to honor the gods.

Roman soldiers were watching Cleopatra closely. They knew she might try to escape. But they never could have guessed there would be danger in a fruit basket.

This stone carving of Cleopatra is from the first century B.C.

A Queen and a General

Egypt had other female leaders, such as Queen Hatshepsut, who ruled from 1479 to 1458 B.C., and her great grandmother, Queen Ahmose Nefertari. Ahmose Nefertari received Egypt's highest military awards for bravery and for driving out foreign invaders.

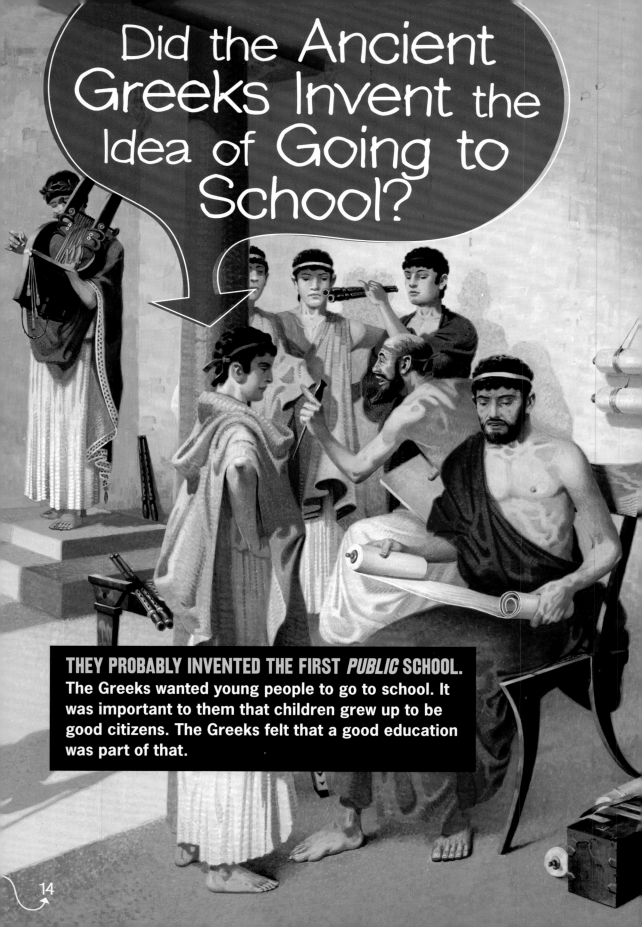

Did the Ancient Greeks Invent the Idea of Going to School?

THEY PROBABLY INVENTED THE FIRST *PUBLIC* SCHOOL. The Greeks wanted young people to go to school. It was important to them that children grew up to be good citizens. The Greeks felt that a good education was part of that.

Boys started school at the age of six or seven. The student's family paid to send him to a tutor, who taught a small group of boys. In the 300s B.C., public schools were opened for families who couldn't afford to pay.

Boys learned to read, quoted poets from memory, and played instruments. They sang, danced, swam, rode horses, wrestled, and ran. Books were expensive, since each one had to be made by hand. The teacher read to the class from one copy, and the class wrote down what the teacher said. School might be held outdoors and at a gymnasium, where the boys exercised.

Girls stayed home and learned to take care of the house. That was hard work in ancient times. Some people thought the world would be better if girls had the same education as boys. But most Greeks considered that idea weird.

Education was handled differently in Sparta. That city was in southern Greece. Sparta was known for its brave warriors. Spartan boys went to military school. They learned music and dancing to make them quick and nimble. That was considered more important than reading and writing. Girls played sports and did exercises. They were expected to become strong, tough mothers.

This bronze statue of a Spartan warrior is from the sixth century B.C.

Throughout Greece, education continued beyond childhood. All their lives, men gathered in the gymnasium to learn new things. They learned from the wisest people of their times, such as Aristotle; his teacher, Plato; and Plato's teacher, Socrates. To this day, people still study their ideas.

Did Socrates Kill Himself by Drinking Poison?

YES. Socrates (469–399 B.C.) taught philosophy in the agora, the marketplace in the center of Athens, Greece. He taught Plato, who taught Aristotle, who taught the famous king Alexander the Great. Socrates didn't write down his own teachings. We know them mostly because of the writings of Plato.

Philosophy is the study of big questions about life. Why are we here? What does it mean to be a good person? What should you do if a law is unfair? Socrates asked questions in a way that made his students think clearly about their answers. Socrates is one of the world's most famous philosophers. But he is also famous for the way he died.

Socrates was a little odd. Sometimes he heard the gods talking to him. Sometimes he didn't seem to believe in any gods at all. He did believe that in order to teach people new ideas, he had to show them that their old ideas were wrong. All this made him seem dangerous and disrespectful to powerful people in Athens. Some said he put ideas about rebellion in young men's heads. For this, Socrates was put on trial and sentenced to death.

His students offered to help him escape, but he turned them down. He said that he had agreed to follow the laws of Athens all the time, not just when it was convenient for him. Socrates was not afraid to die. He believed that his soul would live on and that philosophy prepared him for death.

He died by drinking juice made of a poisonous plant called hemlock (below). The hemlock was probably mixed with poppy and other herbs to make the killer drink very strong. Plato wrote down everything that happened to Socrates after he drank the poison. The story is creepy, but in the end, it was a very peaceful death.

Hemlock comes from the same plant family as carrots, celery, and parsley. That makes it easy to confuse hemlock with tasty vegetables— and end up like Socrates.

This 1787 painting shows the death of Socrates.

Is Mount Olympus a Real Place?

YES. Mount Olympus is the highest mountain in Greece and one of the tallest mountains in Europe. It's 9,570 feet (2,917 meters, or 2 miles) high. When the peak is covered with snow, it can seem to glow. No wonder the ancient Greeks believed the peak was the home of twelve important gods, the Olympians.

Mount Olympus is in northern Greece, near the eastern coast. Zeus, the king of the Greek gods, was said to live there with eleven other gods: Aphrodite, Apollo, Ares, Artemis, Athena, Demeter, Dionysus, Hephaestus, Hera, Hermes, and Poseidon. They drank nectar and ate ambrosia, a food that made them immortal. The god Hephaestus made tables and chairs and golden servants for the Olympians. The furniture and servants moved around on their own. They were like ancient robots!

Modern climbers reached the top of Mount Olympus for the first time in 1913. So far, no one has found the palace of the gods.

To ancient people, the world was a mysterious place. They expected to find gods or spirits in all the most beautiful, most dangerous, or most distant spots. They named many such spots after their gods, including the city of Athens, Greece; the theater of Dionysia in Athens; and the Temple of Apollo at Delphi.

In this image from an ancient Greek cup, the goddess Nike *(second from left)* crowns a human youth *(left)* in front of Zeus *(center)*.

Clever Greeks

There may not have been real robots on Mount Olympus, but the ancient Greeks invented all sorts of mechanical marvels. Heron of Alexandria (A.D. 10-70), like later inventors such as Leonardo da Vinci and Thomas Edison, was constantly thinking of new devices. He created a vending machine and doors that opened on their own. He made puppets that could act out an entire play, complete with sound effects.

Were the First Olympic Games Really Held in Ancient Greece?

YES. The ancient Olympics were held in honor of Zeus. They were not named after Mount Olympus, the home of the gods. They were named after Olympia, the city in western Greece where the first games were held.

For a thousand years, the Olympics were held every four years. The games started as footraces. The first winner ever was a man named Koroibos in 776 B.C. More events were added, such as boxing, chariot racing, and the pentathlon. The pentathlon was five contests: wrestling, running, long jump, javelin throwing, and discus toss. The games also included a fighting match called the *pankration*. In the pankration, opponents could punch or kick one another anywhere and anyhow. Olympic winners received crowns made from olive leaves. They were treated like superstars and sometimes given free meals for life.

Only men and boys who were born free (that is, who had never been slaves) and who spoke Greek were allowed to compete. Married women weren't even allowed to watch. Most competitions were held in the nude to show off healthy bodies and to prove that the athletes were male. Once, a woman named Callipateira disguised herself as a sports trainer so she could see her son compete. After she was discovered, even trainers had to take off their clothes to prove they were men.

The ancient games ended in A.D. 393. The Olympics were not held again until 1896. The new Olympics became an event for everyone in the world.

A Very Long Race

The marathon, a 26-mile (42-kilometer) race, was not part of the ancient Olympics. In 490 B.C., the Persian army invaded a Greek town called Marathon. A messenger named Pheidippides (or Eukles) ran from Marathon to Athens to announce that the Greeks had beaten the Persians. He ran so far and so fast that he died on the spot *(above)*. The distance he ran is the basis for the modern marathon.

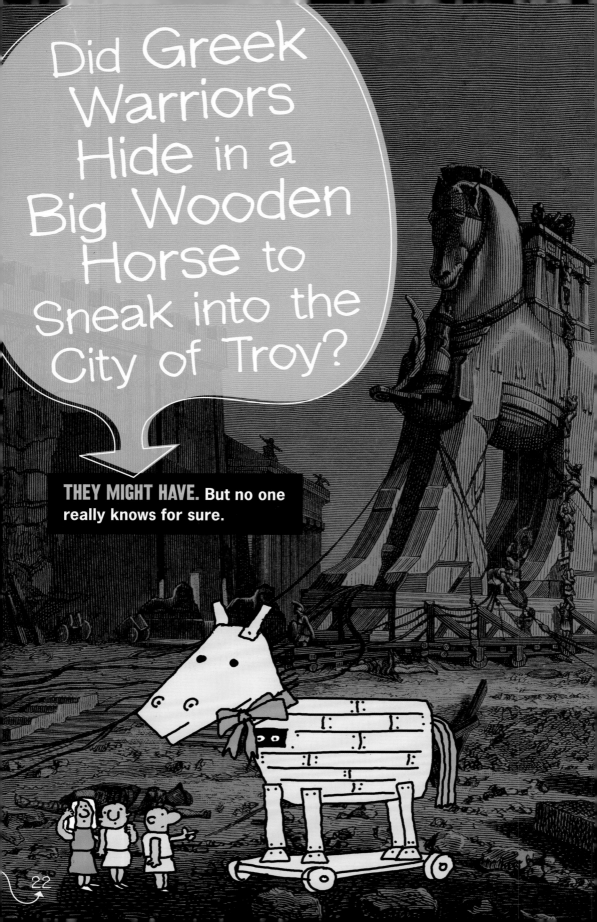

Did Greek Warriors Hide in a Big Wooden Horse to Sneak into the City of Troy?

THEY MIGHT HAVE. But no one really knows for sure.

The Greek poet Homer (who probably lived in the 800s B.C.) wrote the *Iliad* and the *Odyssey*. Those poems describe a war and its aftermath. Homer said the ancient Greeks spent many years attacking Troy, a city in modern-day Turkey.

The Greeks couldn't get past Troy's high, thick walls. So according to Homer, they decided to try a trick. They built a wooden horse and left it outside the city's main gate, as if it were a present for the gods. Then all the Greek soldiers pretended to leave.

The Trojans were suspicious. But they brought the wooden horse into the city anyway and locked the gates again. They didn't know that the horse wasn't empty. In the middle of the night, Greek soldiers climbed out of the horse, opened the gates, and let the rest of the Greek army into Troy. The soldiers destroyed the city. From then on, people would say, "Beware of Greeks bearing gifts."

Judging by the *Iliad*, the Trojan War took place about 1180 B.C. But did the war really happen? After many centuries passed, it was hard to say. Troy didn't survive into modern times, so there wasn't much evidence to go on.

But then, in A.D. 1871, archaeologists Frank Calvert and Heinrich Schliemann discovered the ruins of a city close to where Troy was supposed to have stood. Schliemann found clues that the city had been destroyed by war in about 1180 B.C.! That matched Homer's story. It was evidence that the Trojan War was real.

But what about the Trojan horse? No archaeologist has ever found any pieces of the big wooden horse.

Schliemann found this gold cup while searching the ruins of Mycenae, an ancient Greek city.

Heroic Memories

Homer's *Iliad* is sixteen thousand lines long. In ancient contests, performers had to recite it from memory, starting at any line. Some might get the exciting parts. Others might have to recite nothing but the names of the thousand Greek ships that sailed to Troy.

Did the Roman Emperor Nero Play His Violin While Rome Burned?

NOPE. Ancient Romans didn't even have violins.

This scene from *Quo Vadis*, a 1951 film set in ancient Rome, shows Nero *(center)* playing music as Rome burns.

This is a Roman carving of Nero from the first century A.D.

Nero became emperor when he was only sixteen years old. He enjoyed being in charge, but he also wanted to sing poetry and play the lyre (a type of harp). Singing in public was not considered a dignified hobby, but Nero didn't care. He did whatever he wanted. He was stubborn and cruel. He even had his mother murdered so that he could rule without her.

In A.D. 64, a huge fire burned in Rome for nine days. People woke every day to black skies and smoke. The fire might have started by accident. Romans used a lot of olive oil, for cooking, in lamps, and to clean themselves. They stored large jars of it everywhere. Olive oil burns easily.

Parts of the city were crowded with wooden buildings, so fires spread quickly.

A rumor went around that Nero hadn't tried to stop the fire. Maybe he was more interested in singing than sending out soldiers to fight the blaze. Under pressure, Nero needed someone else to blame. Followers of a new religion called Christianity were accused of setting the fires.

Nero didn't rule for long after that. He had been so cruel during his fourteen years as emperor that the Senate (Rome's government) declared him a public enemy.

The expression "Nero fiddled while Rome burned" is not exactly true. But we still use this phrase when someone in charge does nothing to help while everything falls apart.

Catacombs

Stories and movies tell of early Christians holding secret meetings in Rome's catacombs. Catacombs are underground burial chambers. They were dark and smelly. It's not likely that Christians met down there. But people who wanted to hide for a short time might have gone into the catacombs. After all, no one would have wanted to go there to look for them!

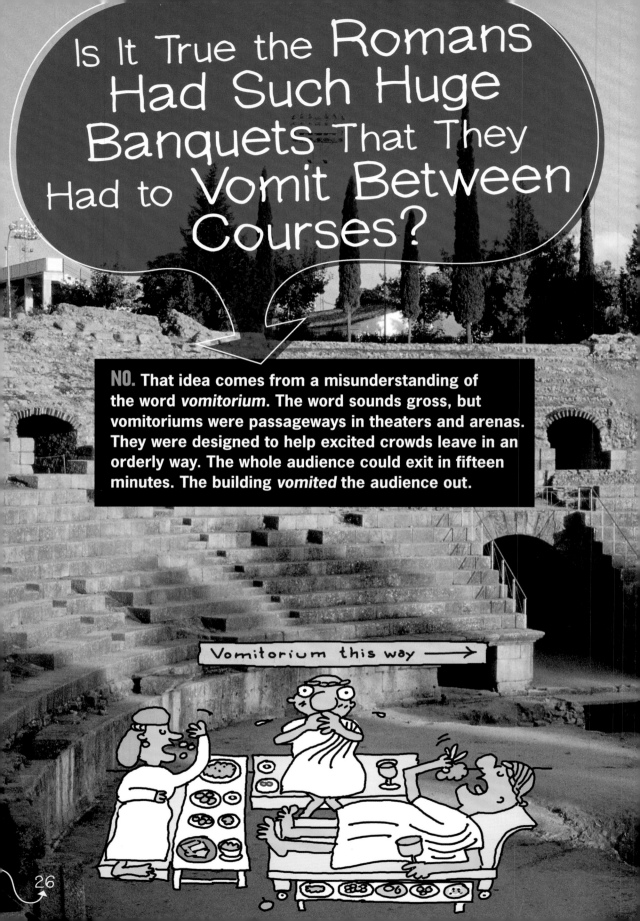

Is It True the Romans Had Such Huge Banquets That They Had to Vomit Between Courses?

NO. That idea comes from a misunderstanding of the word *vomitorium*. The word sounds gross, but vomitoriums were passageways in theaters and arenas. They were designed to help excited crowds leave in an orderly way. The whole audience could exit in fifteen minutes. The building *vomited* the audience out.

Vomitorium this way ⟶

Ancient writers do talk about people who threw up at meals. The writers disapproved of people who wasted food and who drank too much. And there's a report about how Julius Caesar told his dinner host that he was planning to vomit later after eating such a big meal. But if Caesar wanted to throw up, the house had a special place for it, just as modern homes do—a toilet.

Romans loved dinner parties (below). One piece of advice for cooks was that people shouldn't know what they were eating. Romans sometimes ate the same thing over and over, so they disguised it. They'd make a ham look like a chicken. Then they put a sauce made from fermented fish guts, called garum, on almost everything. They used it the way modern people use salt or ketchup. During meals, Romans threw bones and crumbs on the floor. If they suddenly got sick and couldn't move fast enough, that went on the floor too.

But vomiting in the vomitorium? This one's just a joke.

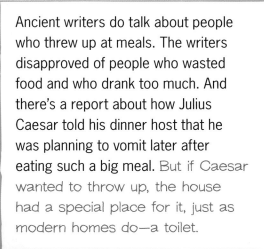

A Roman Cookie Recipe

Take 8 ounces flour, 2 ounces cooking oil, 2 ounces grated cheese, 1 teaspoon cumin, 1 teaspoon aniseed, 3 tablespoons grape juice, and a half teaspoon dried yeast. (Romans didn't use dried yeast, but their grape juice provided some naturally.) Mix it all up. Make cookie shapes on a pan lined with a layer of bay leaves. Bake the cookies at 350°F (177°C) until lightly browned. Have your servants repeat the process until they get it right. Then serve the cookies to the emperor.

Did Hannibal March Elephants across the Alps to Attack Rome?

YES, he did—all the way from Spain!

Hannibal was the oldest son of a general from Carthage named Hamilcar Barca. Hamilcar fought a long war against the Romans. It was called the First Punic War (264–241 B.C.). Carthage is in North Africa, but the Carthaginians spread all around the Mediterranean Sea and into Iberia. (Iberia was the Roman name for Spain.) Hannibal even married an Iberian princess.

Like his father, Hannibal became a general. And like his father, he wanted to destroy Rome. In 218 B.C., Hannibal attacked towns that were allies of the Romans. The Romans declared the Second Punic War (218–201 B.C.).

Hannibal decided to invade Italy. He marched over the Pyrenees (the mountains between Spain and France) with his army and thirty-seven elephants. The elephants were carried over rivers on large rafts. Finally, Hannibal, his army, and his elephants crossed the snowy Alps (the mountains that run through central Europe). The trip was hard on the soldiers but harder on the elephants. By the time Hannibal reached southern Italy, he had only one elephant left.

Hannibal defeated several Roman legions (military units). He expected Rome's allies to surrender. To his surprise, Rome's friends stayed loyal. Maybe they knew that Roman law would be better than the harsh Carthaginian rulers. Slowly, the Romans and their allies pushed Hannibal's army south. A young Roman commander, Publius Cornelius Scipio, attacked the city of Carthage itself. He won the war.

Rome's determination was stronger than all of Hannibal's elephants. If more elephants had survived the trip over the Alps, maybe Hannibal would have won the war. Then we'd talk about the Carthaginian Empire—and not the Roman Empire—as one of the greatest powers in history.

These ancient Carthaginian ruins are in Tunisia, a country in North Africa.

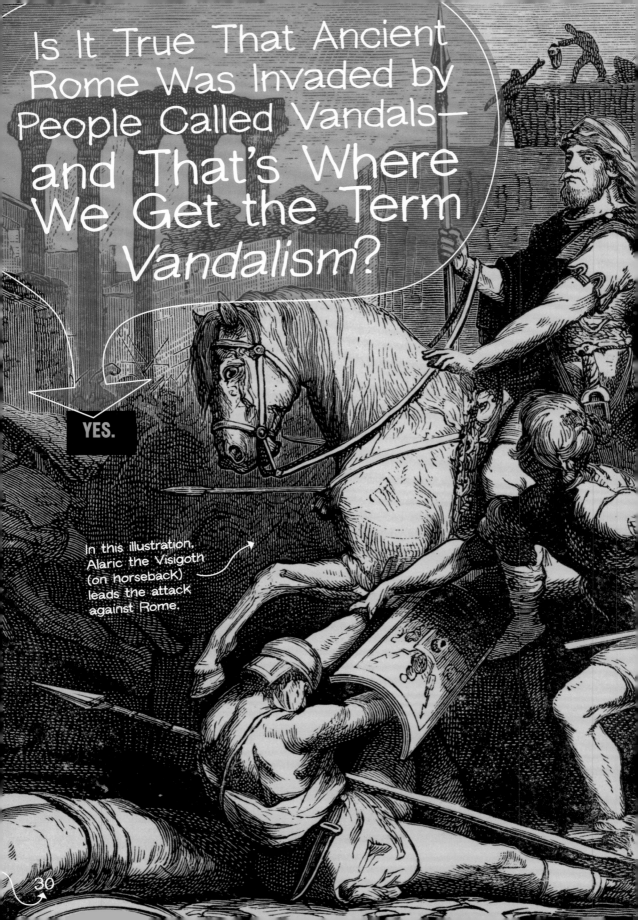

Is It True That Ancient Rome Was Invaded by People Called Vandals— and That's Where We Get the Term *Vandalism?*

YES.

In this illustration, Alaric the Visigoth (on horseback) leads the attack against Rome.

The Vandals were a Germanic tribe from north of the Roman Empire. Other tribes from the same area included the Visigoths and the Ostrogoths. For centuries, the Roman Empire ruled many different groups of people. People didn't like Rome's wars and high taxes. But mostly, everyone cooperated with the empire. Until the fifth century.

Warriors from outside the empire, such as Attila the Hun, began eyeing the rich city of Rome. Soon those warriors became too strong for Rome to keep them out. Alaric the Visigoth attacked Rome in A.D. 410. His men destroyed the tombs of the old emperors, but the city survived.

Meanwhile, the Vandals spread around the Mediterranean.

Visigoths were here

They were raiders and pirates. In June 455, *they* attacked the city of Rome.

By the fifth century, Rome had Christian rulers and a pope. Pope Leo I begged the Vandals not to kill anyone, but he couldn't stop them from looting. Vandals stormed through the city for fourteen days. They stole treasures and captured many people. They sold the captives as slaves in Africa.

This was truly the last blow to the city of Rome. The western half of the Roman Empire began to fall apart. It was the end of ancient times and the beginning of the Middle Ages. It must have seemed like the "dark ages" to the people of Rome.

In their own language, the Vandals' name meant "wanderers." In modern English, *vandalism* is the word for damaging someone else's property or destroying something beautiful and old.

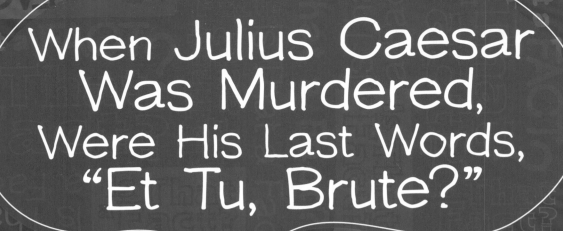

When Julius Caesar Was Murdered, Were His Last Words, "Et Tu, Brute?"

NO. This is a very famous quote. "Et tu, Brute?" is Latin (the language of ancient Rome). It means "And you too, Brutus?" English writer William Shakespeare uses the phrase in his play *Julius Caesar*. But Caesar didn't really say those words.

In Caesar's day, Rome's government was run by senators and elected officials. Caesar was a very powerful army general. Some of the senators were afraid he would take over the government and declare himself king. They decided to stop him. In 44 B.C., on March 15—called the Ides of March—a group of men gathered. Then, armed with knives, they attacked Caesar. When Caesar saw his friend Brutus among his attackers, he gave up fighting.

Shakespeare took the phrase "Et tu, Brute?" from the ancient historian Suetonius—more or less. Upper-class Romans spoke Greek as easily as they spoke Latin. It was a sign of being educated and having good manners. In Greek, says Suetonius, Caesar's words were "*Kai su, teknon?*" That means "You too, my child?" Some Romans believed Brutus was Caesar's secret son. Caesar's dying words were the proof!

But Suetonius also wrote that Caesar *probably* said nothing at all. Knowing the facts never stopped Suetonius from reporting rumors. He knew that readers always want gossip about famous people. So "Et tu, Brute?" went down in history. People still say the phrase when someone they trust hurts them.

Lend Me Your Ears

Shakespeare wrote that at Caesar's funeral, his second-in-command, Mark Antony, gave a speech. It starts, "Friends, Romans, countrymen, lend me your ears. . . ." Historians know that Antony did give a speech in real life. And he was a brilliant speaker. His words made the citizens so angry they turned against Caesar's enemies. But no copy exists of what he really said. He's lucky to have someone like Shakespeare for a ghost writer.

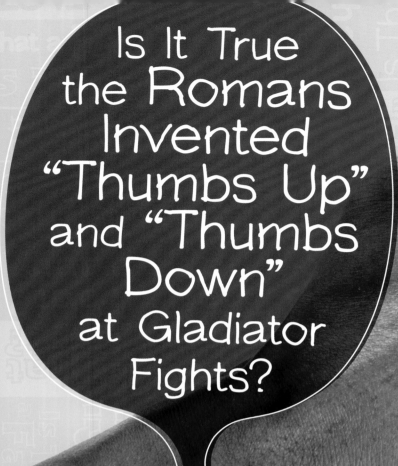

Is It True the Romans Invented "Thumbs Up" and "Thumbs Down" at Gladiator Fights?

IT'S HALF TRUE.

One scene happens a lot in movies about ancient Rome. At the end of a gladiator fight, the winner looks into the crowd. The emperor, in a golden wreath and purple robes, holds his hand out and turns his thumb down. Too bad for the loser! That means death. Or the emperor turns his thumb up, and the loser is freed. But that's only in the movies.

Instead, Romans used a closed fist, with the thumb pressed against the other fingers, to show mercy and let the loser live. They also waved white handkerchiefs and shouted. The sign the loser didn't want to

see was thumbs up! It was more like a baseball umpire's signal for "you're out!"

Fights were held on religious holidays, in honor of a famous person or to celebrate winning a war. Gladiators were slaves or volunteers who couldn't find other work. Women could become gladiators too. Gladiators fought one another, criminals, and wild animals. Criminals were expected to fight to the death. For them, a gladiator fight was an execution.

Other gladiators could earn their freedom after winning a certain number of fights. They were as famous as modern sports stars or professional wrestlers. It took a lot of training to become a good gladiator. People who ran gladiatorial schools didn't want their best fighters to kill one another— except on very special occasions. Many fights ended with a closed fist for mercy.

Did You Know?

Titus Flavius Vespasianus (usually just called Vespasian) became emperor in A.D. 69. He started building the biggest sports arena Rome had ever seen. It was called the Colosseum. As many as sixty-eight thousand people could fit inside. It was even flooded at least once to stage battles between ships.

This seventeenth-century French painting shows Vespasian giving orders to workers building the Roman Colosseum.

Did Ancient People Really Believe the Gods Could Appear on Earth at Any Time?

YES. Stories tell about gods visiting humans, sneaking up on them, or eavesdropping when they said something bad. It's not an odd idea. Many people in modern times believe angels or other good spirits visit human beings.

Ancient people believed gods were sometimes cruel and sometimes kind. In other words, they were just like humans but much more powerful. Not only did the gods visit, but they also often had children with humans. These half-human, half-god offspring often became heroes. Heroes were figures in ancient stories who performed amazing acts.

This Greek vase from the fifth century B.C. shows the half-human, half-god son of Zeus—Hercules.

People also believed that the gods sent messages to humans. Many believed that the gods spoke through kings, emperors, and other rulers. Greeks also traveled long distances to get advice from oracles in places where gods lived. Oracles were priests and priestesses who repeated the gods' messages, usually in riddles.

Romans might have been harder to convince. Or maybe they believed that stories about gods mixing with humans only happened very long ago. Julius Caesar could say he was descended from Venus, and people might reply, "I guess that could be true."

But Romans did believe that gods spoke by leaving hints and clues—called omens—everywhere. They believed their ancestors watched over them, so they built miniature temples for them. Deceased emperors were supposed to watch over the Romans too. Romans built big stone temples for the dead rulers.

Emperor Vespasian didn't believe any of it. His last words, in A.D. 79, were a joke. Right before he died, he muttered, "I think I'm becoming a god!"

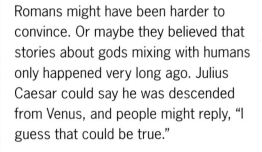

GLOSSARY

alabaster: a smooth, white mineral used to make statues, vases, and lamps

barge: a flat-bottomed boat used for traveling a river such as the Nile in Egypt. Cleopatra had a golden barge.

bitumen: a black substance made from coal or petroleum. Bitumen is part of the asphalt and tar used on roads.

catacomb: a network of underground burial chambers

Colosseum: the gladiator arena built by the Roman emperor Vespasian and his sons, Titus and Domitian. It was sometimes spelled "Coliseum."

garum: a sauce made from fermented fish guts that was used by the Romans on their food

gymnasium: a place where Greeks exercised and discussed ideas. The word *gymnasium* comes from the Greek word for naked, because Greeks usually exercised in the nude.

legion: a unit of the Roman army with about five thousand men. Each legion had a Roman numeral and a name, such as I Italica and III Cyrenaica.

lyre: an ancient type of small harp

nectar: a wine made with honey that the Greek gods drank

omen: a hint or event that can be seen as either a good or bad sign. Lightning or a flock of birds flying overhead are examples of ancient omens.

oracle: a priest or a priestess who gave advice and predictions from the gods

pankration: a no-holds-barred fighting match in the ancient Olympics. Opponents were allowed to do anything but stick fingers in one another's eyes, noses, or mouths.

pentathlon: an athletic contest with five different events

philosophy: the study of big questions about life, the world, beauty, and how people treat one another. It means "love of wisdom."

resin: a sticky substance made by trees that dries very hard. Amber is a type of resin.

shabtis: small figures made of clay or wood that were buried with mummies. They were believed to come to life and do work for the mummies.

terra-cotta: a reddish brown clay used for pottery and statues

triumph: a parade in ancient Rome celebrating a victory in battle

SELECTED BIBLIOGRAPHY

Bloch, Enid. "Hemlock Poisoning and the Death of Socrates: Did Plato Tell the Truth?" *Internet Journal of the International Plato Society*, January 2001. http://gramata.univ-paris1.fr/Plato/article9.html (July 17, 2009).

Corbeill, Anthony. *Nature Embodied: Gesture in Ancient Rome*. Princeton, NJ: Princeton University Press, 2004.

Korfmann, Manfred. "Was There a Trojan War?" *Archaeology* 57, no. 3 (May–June 2004). http://www.archaeology.org/0405/etc/troy.html (July 17, 2009).

Strassler, Robert B., ed. *The Landmark Herodotus: The Histories*. Translated by Andrea L. Purvis. New York: Anchor, 2009.

Suetonius. *The Twelve Caesars*. Translated by Robert Graves. London: Penguin Books, 1989.

Watterson, Barbara. *Women in Ancient Egypt*. London: Wrens Park Publishing, 1998.

FURTHER READING

The Ancient Olympics
http://www.perseus.tufts.edu/Olympics
Compare ancient and modern Olympic sports, tour modern Olympia, and read stories about famous ancient Olympic athletes.

BBC Schools: Primary History
http://www.bbc.co.uk/schools/primaryhistory
Explore history through a photo and video library, an interactive timeline, quizzes, activities, and games.

Fontes, Justine, and Ron Fontes. *The Trojan Horse: The Fall of Troy*. Minneapolis: Graphic Universe, 2007. This graphic novel tells the story of the Greeks' victory over the Trojans.

Kidipede
http://www.historyforkids.org
Read about human history from start to finish and get homework help on this website created by a history professor.

Limke, Jeff. *Isis & Osiris: To the Ends of the Earth*. Minneapolis: Graphic Universe, 2007. This graphic novel recounts the ancient Egyptian myth of Osiris, the first mummy.

Pearson, Anne. *Ancient Greece*. New York: DK, 2007. Check out this title for more information on ancient Greece.

Sonneborn, Liz. *The Egyptians: Life in Ancient Egypt*. Minneapolis: Millbrook Press, 2010. This title details ancient Egyptians' daily activities, religion, buildings, inventions, and leaders.

INDEX

ACKNOWLEDGMENTS
The images in this book are used with the permission of:
© Murat Taner/Photographer's Choice/Getty Images, pp. 1, 4;
The Art Archive/Egyptian Museum Cairo/Gianni Dagli Orti, pp. 2
(top), 6; © Robert Harding Picture Library/SuperStock, pp. 2
(bottom), 10, 12 (bottom); © Stock Montage/SuperStock, pp. 3,
22–23, 33; The Art Archive/Musée du Louvre Paris/Gianni Dagli
Orti, pp. 5 (both), 19, 37; The Art Archive/Gianni Dagli Orti,
pp. 6–7, 16–17; © DEA/S. Vannini/De Agostini Picture Library/
Getty Images, pp. 8–9; © Robert Harding World Imagery/
Getty Images, p. 9; The Art Archive/Musée Archéologique
Naples/Gianni Dagli Orti, pp. 11, 27; © Yamini Chao/Stone/
Getty Images, pp. 12–13; The Art Archive, pp. 13, 30–31;
The Art Archive/H.M. Herget/NGS Image Collection, p. 14;
© Ancient Art and Architecture Collection Ltd/Alamy, p. 15;
© Adisa/Dreamstime.com, p. 17 (top); © North Wind Picture
Archives, p. 17 (bottom); © Piotr Tomicki/Dreamstime.com,
p. 18; © Mary Evans Picture Library/Douglas McCarthy/The
Image Works, p. 20; The Art Archive/Museo di Villa Giulia Rome/
Gianni Dagli Orti, p. 21 (top); © Rischgitz/Hulton Archive/Getty
Images, p. 21 (bottom); The Art Archive/Musée des Beaux Arts
Besancon/Gianni Dagli Orti, p. 23 (top); © William West/AFP/
Getty Images, p. 23 (bottom); MGM/The Kobal Collection, p. 24;
The Art Archive/Staatliche Glypothek Munich/Alfredo Dagli Orti,
p. 25; © Quim Llenas/Hulton Archive/Getty Images, pp. 26–27;
© Bettmann/CORBIS, p. 28; © Steve Vidler/SuperStock,
p. 29; The Art Archive/Museum der Stadt Wien/Gianni Dagli
Orti, pp. 32–33; © Geerart/Dreamstime.com, p. 34 (top);
© Antartis/Dreamstime.com, p. 34 (bottom); The Art Archive/
Musée du Château de Versailles/Gianni Dagli Orti, p. 35; © Larry
Dunmire/SuperStock, pp. 36–37.

Front cover: © Murat Taner/Photographer's Choice/Getty
Images; © iStockphoto.com/Robert Kerton (figures).

Text and illustrations copyright © 2011 by Lerner Publishing
Group, Inc.

Lerner Publications Company
A division of Lerner Publishing Group, Inc.
241 First Avenue North
Minneapolis, MN 55401 U.S.A.

Website address: www.lernerbooks.com

Library of Congress Cataloging-in-Publication Data

Burrell, Carol M. Scavella.
    Did Greek soldiers really hide inside the Trojan horse? :
and other questions about the ancient world / by Carol M.
Scavella Burrell.
        p. cm. — (Is that a fact?)
    Includes bibliographical references and index.
    ISBN 978–0–7613–4912–9 (lib. bdg. : alk. paper)
    1. Civilization, Ancient—Juvenile literature. 2. Egypt—
Juvenile literature. 3. Greece—Juvenile literature. 4.
Rome—Juvenile literature. I. Title.
CB311.B88 2011
930.1—dc22   2010001252

Manufactured in the United States of America
1 – PC – 7/15/10